DEMOCRACY
IN FREEFALL

Restoring Our Freedom Before It's Too Late

DALE HOWARD WRIGHT

Trafford rev. 07/27/2011

 www.trafford.com

North America & International
toll-free: 1 888 232 4444 (USA & Canada)
phone: 250 383 6864 ♦ fax: 812 355 4082

ABOUT THE AUTHOR

During the last four generations Dale Howard Wright and his family have displayed a monumental sense of patriotism and dedication to our country.

During WWII, his father Howard, and his four uncles served in the military with distinction and honor. Three of the brothers, William, Howard and Donald all served with the Army's 132nd Infantry Regiment of the Americal Division on Guadalcanal in support of the 1st Marine Division. Brother Bud also served in the Army, while Ted served in the Coast Guard.

During the next generation, Dale and three of his cousins continued the family's tradition of patriotic military service. Colonel Frank Wright served in the Air Force and piloted more then 400 B-52 bombing sorties during his Vietnam service. Navy Captain Bruce Wright served in several critical assignments on high ranking naval staffs. CWO W4 William Wright became a specialist in handling of classified supplies for the Army. During Operation Desert storm, he was recalled to active duty to again apply his critical knowledge of handling classified materials.

Major Dale Wright served two combat tours with the Army in Vietnam as an Infantry commander. He was decorated with the Silver Star medal, Soldiers Medal for lifesaving, Bronze Star medal, Army Commendation Medal and the Vietnamese Cross of Gallantry for valor. He also received the Purple Heart for combat wounds. All four officers retired with more then twenty years of faithful service to their country.

During the third generation, two of Dale's six children served in the military. Three of his daughters married military husbands. And one of his grandsons, Anthony, is serving in the Army, and was wounded in Iraq.

The Wright family has always served its country with honor and pride. They have always been patriots. Now is the time for all Americans to join with us in restoring our fundamental rights to freedom. This is the driving force that has driven me to write this book.

Dale Howard Wright

DEMOCRACY IN FREEFALL

RESTORING OUR FREEDOM BEFORE ITS TO LATE

BY   DALE HOWARD WRIGHT

FORWARD

I wish to dedicate this book to all of you who have shared your feelings with me about our failed government. We may not always have agreed on a singular approach to ending our plight. But, the main thing is that we identified the problems at hand. These often-heated discussions only served to stir my passion for finding workable solutions.

I also wish to thank both the Wright and Campbell families for their interest, input and support. A special thanks goes out to my Uncle Donald Wright for furnishing numerous intelligent recommendations on how to proceed with this work. Also, I want to thank my friend and personal editor, Eva Frazier, from Blackhawk Technical College, for cleaning this manuscript up. And finally, to my lovely and devoted wife, Denise, who sat through all of those many hours of edits and re-edits, thanks Honey.

In researching this book, I have come to **ONE** startling conclusion. Unless we take positive steps <u>now</u> to end the reign of incompetence by our nation's leadership, we will look to the days of the great depression as days of utopia.

TABLE OF CONTENTS

PART THREE: REVIVING THE ECONOMY, CREATING NEW JOBS AND PRODUCTS

PART FOUR: GREATLY REDUCING CRIME THROUGH HARSHER TREATMENT OF CONVICTED CRIMINALS

INTRODUCTION

Less than three centuries ago, our country fought a war with England to gain its independence. Until recently, we have thrived because of the intelligence and foresight of our founding fathers. Today we face serious problems. If we the people do not take bold actions to alter the course of our Federal Government in Washington, our country's leadership will <u>ultimately lead this nation to destruction and demise.</u>

We are all familiar with the Preamble to the Constitution. It states, "WE THE PEOPLE................" Never before have these three words become more important then now.

The Constitution of the United States allows us to elect representatives to run our Federal Government. These representatives are sworn to serve <u>the people </u>and protect our best interests. However, these very same elected officials, including the Congress and our former and current serving Presidents, have betrayed this sacred trust. They have totally ignored the mandate of the "voice of the people." Many members of Congress, including other high-ranking officials serving in the Executive branch of our government are only interested in furthering their own personal agendas. In many cases, elected officials obtain illegal financial gains from outside interest groups, in exchange for exerting their influence on important legislation.

The voice of the people has been ignored for far too long. The overall effect has resulted in the gross mismanagement of our county's wealth and prosperity. As a result of these actions, we now find our country approaching Bankruptcy, Record Unemployment and a retirement system that will not be able to support future generations of contributors. This must be stopped **NOW** and fiscal responsibility must be restored. It is time for "WE THE PEOPLE" to reclaim our heritage and create a revised order of government which will once again respect and serve its people with honor. Then, and only then, will we show the world that our country truly is a model for Democracy.

This book will address many of the problems that must be changed in order to restore our freedom. Let me be perfectly clear, I am not seeking office. **Also, in no way do I suggest or support any form of violent revolution against our Government.** Instead, I propose a peaceful reorganization of the Federal Government. These changes, when instituted by

"WE THE PEOPLE," will once again restore our Democratic way of life and end the Socialistic government that now rules us. One of the most important changes that I propose is to establish a new fourth branch of government. This branch will be called the Oversight Branch. Its purpose will be to put restraints on the actions of Congress. This branch will be discussed in detail in a separate chapter.

Another critical change will be how major legislation is processed and voted upon. In the future, **all major legislation** that significantly effects our society or world affairs **must** be voted on by **popular vote of the people.** Congress will still be expected to debate important legislation and these debates will be presented to the public prior to the scheduled date for action by popular vote. In this way, we will no longer be ruled arbitrarily by the political vote of a few administrative assistants known as Congressmen and Senators. The **popular vote will become the law of the land** and freedom will be restored to our people.

So many Americans today feel helpless to do anything to improve their plight. They see no end to the shrinking dollar, unemployment and the continuous burden of new taxes. Who can they turn to for help? The answer is simple, but first I will tell you whom they cannot turn to and why.

If you look to our elected officials in Washington for help, forget it. Most of the Senate is made up of lawyers and they are experts in knowing how to perform in front of a group to get elected. I have no vendetta against lawyers. In fact, my son is a very good and honorable one. However, the country has been duped into thinking that our congressional representatives can help you in any way. First, think of this: there are approximately 550 Congressmen and Senators who serve in the Congress and the Administration. These are our duly elected representatives sent to Washington to insure that our population of three hundred ten million citizens is served with honor and trust. These officials are expected to make their decisions in our best interest. However, were our best interests served when Congress wound up sending thousands of good paying manufacturing jobs to other countries as a result of NAFTA? Should our retirees, who rely on their meager monthly social security checks, be happy when they have not received an increase for the past two years? For the record, health care and prescription drug costs have continued to increase causing our seniors retirement incomes to shrink even more. Also, should we be happy that our country's leadership refuses to deport illegal immigrants? Don't forget that these immigrants take jobs away that are desperately needed by our legal population. These are just a few of the topics that will be addressed further.

The reason that our best interests are not being acted on is because the Congress is vested with men and women who spend millions of dollars to get elected and millions more to get re-elected. Understand that each congressman owes his or her loyalty to the party or individuals and corporations, who put up the money for their campaign. To our elected representatives, your individual vote is almost a joke. They are campaigning to win a popularity contest. If they look neat and clean and suggest that they will work towards bringing more jobs to your state, they will likely get elected. But if they took a lie detector test and were asked if they would <u>always</u> vote in accordance with the desires of their constituency, they would fail every time. Also, remember that they are members of either the Republican or Democratic Parties. They will further act and vote in support of their party's desires, regardless of personal feelings. So now you are getting an idea of why our political system no longer serves the people.

If we continue to let the infamous 550 from Washington rule us; we could wind up like the citizens of Germany did, in the 1930's, when Hitler took over. Please don't laugh. I'm serious. Follow the German people's path into National Socialism and you will find marked similarities with the path that our government is following today.

I said that the answer to solving our problems is a simple one. First of all, do you know what the two most feared words in Washington are? The two words are "**POPULAR VOTE.**" By my math, our population of three hundred ten million people represents a lot more then the 550 officials elected to Congress and the White House that make all of the decisions. So I propose that we start a new party that is non-political in nature. Let's call ourselves "**We the People Party**" for now. We will start from grass roots with a branch in every county or parish in the country. We will resemble our forefathers and be **made up of volunteers and patriots to the core**. We will select our candidates from **true Americans** who are highly educated in the fields of economics or who have strong engineering and production skills. Within four years, we will control the House of Representatives and within eight years, we will control the Senate and the Congress as a whole.

Our actions will never pose a threat to our governmental structure because we will be enacting the will of the majority of the people. Additionally, fiscal control will be restored by the Oversight Branch's restrictive powers over congressional spending. And again, the **popular vote** will be used for all major legislative actions. **This is the only way for us to peacefully restore our nation to its former greatness.**

Some of the topics in this book are mine alone. However, most of the problems have come from my friends, who, feeling helpless to affect change, have shared their feelings with me. I don't profess to have all of the answers, **but somewhere in this vast and glorious country of ours we have educated people from all walks of life, who will stand up and come forward. These modern day patriots will lead us on the path to restore freedom and prosperity for all.**

Now is the time for the people to become involved in saving this country and insuring that we protect our heritage for centuries to come. No longer can you or I delay by just taking what is given to us. I am a patriot and I believe that "**THE LORD HELPS THOSE WHO HELP THEMSELVES.**" **It is your turn to join with us in becoming a Patriot too.**

Become part of the new movement to restore freedom for you and your family. Remember that this is our last chance to stop "DEMOCRACY IN FREEFALL."

CHAPTER 1

"We the People Party" Taking Control of Our Destiny

In this chapter we will discuss how "We the People Party" can once again regain control of our country. We can expect to be fought at every turn by the Washington establishment, but if we have the resolve to restore our freedom, nothing can stop us. It is time to rid us of a decaying system of government that no longer serves the best interests of the people. It is time to remove members of Congress who serve only themselves and the special interest groups that provide them with financial support. In my eyes, they have betrayed the people of this country, whom they are duty bound to serve. You can expect these congressmen to use every dirty trick that they know to insure that we don't succeed, **BUT WE WILL SUCCEED.**

It is time to take charge and put an end to unjust legislation that cripples our economy and ultimately takes food from our tables. What happens when oxygen is removed from a fire? The fire disappears. The same principle will work by removing our ineffective and crooked congressmen from office.

It is time for all of us to stand up and be counted as we become modern day **patriots of our nation.**

But first, we all need to undergo a major attitude adjustment. The time has come to take a serious look at ourselves. We have become a nation of **"ZOMBIES"**. We walk around in a haze, complaining to our family and friends about how we are abused by our government. Yet in reality, we are helpless to do anything about our plight. So we go on day after day and year after year watching as our freedom continues to be usurped by our elected representatives serving in Washington. If you think that things are bad now, <u>just keep watching and waiting a little longer.</u> It will get a lot worse financially for you and your family in the very near future **<u>unless we take action now.</u>**

Every other year is an election year. You are asked to vote for candidates to serve as **"YOUR"** representatives in Washington. I applaud those of you who still take an interest in <u>trying</u> to choose the best man or woman possible for the job. However, it should be noted that once these people are elected and go to Washington, they immediately find out that they have **<u>no more power to affect change than you or me.</u>** So they began doing the most important thing on their agenda. They started preparing to get re-elected. This is called job security.

So, what can "We the People Party" do to put and end to the mess that has been created in Washington over these many years of failure by both political parties? In theory, it is very simple. However, in execution it will be time consuming and will require the voluntary support of many dedicated patriots. This book will act as a guide for directing us once again on our path to freedom.

First, we will need to develop an organization for the purpose of getting the true word out to the people. One dedicated retiree in each county or parish, who shares the passion of restoring freedom to the people, is enough to get started. Like lighting a match to dry weeds, word of our movement will spread like wild fire, until we ignite the entire country. With a pool of approximately two hundred million legal voters, we can and will achieve our goals by first **removing** our ineffective congressmen in Washington, and then **replacing them with our candidates.** A draft organizational chart for the new party is shown at Tab A.

So for openers, lets call our party "We the People Party." We will be forever known as the party of the common man and woman. Initially our goals should be as follows:

1)   To insure that we have a firm voice in choosing our posterity by use of the popular vote for all elections and major legislation that affects our population as a whole.

2)   To select highly qualified candidates to serve as our representatives in Congress. These elected officials will be sworn to serve the best interests of the voice of the people and not that of any other outside influence.

TAB A

ORGANIZATIONAL CHART

"We the People Party"

PARTY FOR THE COMMON MAN AND WOMAN

```
                    ┌─────────────────────┐
                    │   "We the People"   │
                    │   National Party    │
                    │    Headquarters     │
                    └──────────┬──────────┘
                               │
                    ┌──────────┴──────────┐
                    │    State Office     │
                    └──────────┬──────────┘
        ┌──────┬──────┬────────┴────────┬──────┬──────┐
    ┌───────┐ ┌───────┐ ┌──────────────┐ ┌───────┐ ┌───────┐
    │       │ │       │ │County or Parish│ │       │ │       │
    │       │ │       │ │     Office     │ │       │ │       │
    └───────┘ └───────┘ └──────────────┘ └───────┘ └───────┘
```

3)   As our representatives, these honorable servants of the people will advise us on the pros and cons of pending legislation so we may make the best choices when we go to the polls to cast our popular vote.

4)   To ratify changes to the Constitution of the United States establishing the "popular vote" as the means for determining the final outcome of a piece of major legislation.

5)   To ratify changes to the Constitution establishing a
        fourth branch of the U.S. Government. This branch
        will serve as a check and balance over Congress to insure
        that the will of the people is enforced. It will be known
        as the Oversight Branch.

One of our primary goals must be to establish the
Oversight Branch so that we can insure that Congress stays in
check. This branch will be totally non-political in nature and
it will always support the voice of the people. Staffing and
mission responsibilities for this branch will be discussed in the
next chapter.

Also of extreme importance, is to get legislation passed
authorizing the use of the popular vote for important matters
affecting our society as a whole. We can expect major resistance
from the other two parties. One of their arguments will
probably be that using computers as voting machines to process
the popular vote won't work. They will say that computers are
unreliable, insecure and an unnecessary expense. **But the
truth is that we will process the popular vote significantly
faster by the simple use of a secure network**. Today we live in
an advanced communications era. Computer technology with
its speed and responsiveness now gives us the tools to establish

and process the "popular vote." The popular vote will be the method used for approving major legislation. If this technology had existed during the drafting of the original Constitution, our forefathers would surely have given the vote to the people.

Just think, no more "hanging chads" or endless time consuming recounts of paper ballots. For the cost of a few computer terminals to replace the old voting machines, processing time will be greatly reduced. By ending the use of printed ballots, the savings will soon pay for the terminals. As for security, don't forget that our military, law enforcement and governmental agencies all use forms of secure computer networks. We can also use a similar secure system for use in processing the popular vote.

I am sure that the states will have to ratify these changes to the United States Constitution, but we **must** first have approval for use of the popular vote during the ratification process. **Without the popular vote, we will still be at the mercy of the failed political system.**

Support for our goals will no doubt require signatures on petitions. If it calls for 100,000 signatures we will get 1,000,000 signatures. This will definitely strike fear into the hearts of our current elected officials. Those congressmen who fail to support us in this endeavor, can rest assured that their political careers will be finished at the end of their term in office. The voters of "We the People Party" will insure that they are voted out of office by sheer weight of votes cast. Remember that seldom does the nation record 55% of its eligible voters for a presidential election. This means that "We the People Party" can draw from the other 45% that failed to vote. Additionally, we will gain a large number of disgruntled voters from the other two major parties, when they realize that this time their vote will count.

Every plan should have a backup. If we are initially unsuccessful in attaining our goals, we will fight back and **WIN**. With our strong voting base, "We the People Party" will ultimately elect all new representatives to replace those currently in office, including the President. Then we can effect legislation to correct all of Congress's wrong doings. **Our** representatives to Congress will pass legislation leading to approving the popular vote. **This is called restoring Democracy to the people.**

In order to support this organization we will require financial support from our members. We will only be asking for voluntary contributions of $5.00 per member. These funds will be used for administrative expenses. Each new member will be asked to register by filling out a short registration form listing his or her name, address, and telephone number and email address. Each new member will receive a colorful campaign button stating that "I AM A PATRIOT." As our membership grows, won't it be wonderful seeing our party's buttons being worn everywhere? Hopefully, this will also encourage others to join our ranks. With the support of the people, our movement's membership will easily eclipse that of the other parties, thus insuring that the candidates of "We the People Party" win at the poles.

IN ENDING THIS CHAPTER, PLEASE NOTE THAT, WE <u>MUST GET APPROVAL FOR THE POPULAR VOTE.</u> WITHOUT THE VOTE WE WILL NEVER WIN SUPPORT OVER THE 550 POLITITIONS IN WASHINGTON, WHO FORCE THEIR WILL ON US.

HOWEVER, WE HAVE A BACKUP PLAN THAT CAN'T FAIL. SO FASTEN YOUR SEAT BELTS. WE THE PEOPLE ARE ABOUT TO REGAIN OUR FREEDOM AND EXPEL THOSE WHO HAVE USURPED OUR RIGHTS FOR SO LONG.

CHAPTER 2

The New Oversight Branch of the Federal Government

Purpose: The purpose of creating a new fourth branch of the Federal Government is to provide a non-political branch which will insure that Congress acts **only** in accordance with the mandate of people. No longer will congressmen have the power to ignore the will of the people. Neither will they be allowed to vote strictly along their party's line, nor in support of some special interest groups that feed their re-election war chests with bogus contributions.

Primary Responsibilities: The Oversight Branch of the Federal Government, hereafter referred to as the (OBFG), will be tasked with the following authority and responsibilities. A table of organization is shown at Tab B.

The Department of Congressional Oversight and Review (DCOR) is tasked with the most important roles. They are responsible for insuring that Congress operates in accordance with the will of the people at all times. The DCOR is thus the check and balance to keep Congress under control. Prior to any bill being sent to the Congress for debate, the review element of DCOR will be responsible for reviewing it in minute detail. This will serve several purposes.

First, they will insure that the bill is clean of any amendments that may have arbitrarily been added. This is a common practice used throughout the

TAB B

ORGANIZATIONAL CHART

OVERSIGHT BRANCH OF THE FEDERAL GOVERNMENT

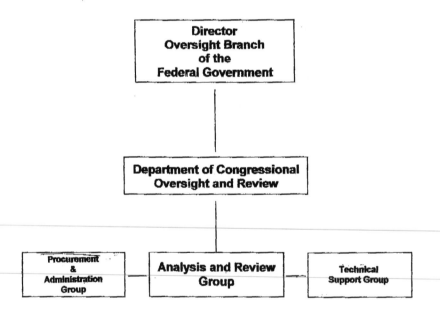

Congress that allows a congressman to add one of his favorite projects to a bill in return for his vote. In most cases, the amendment has nothing to do with the primary bill at all. This sneaky practice will not be condoned and it will be nipped it in the bud. Contempt of Congress citations will be enforced against any congressman who attempts to defraud the people he serves.

Once the bill is reviewed it will be sent to a review board to determine its Category status. If it is considered routine legislation, it will be designated as a Class II bill. Class II bills will be processed by the Congress to completion. This will include signature by the President.

If a bill has a significant effect on the American society or it impacts on world affairs, it will be classified as Class I. It will then be deferred for final action by popular vote of the people. Samples of these Categories are:

Class I

A bill proposing the repeal of trade agreements such as NAFTA.

A bill proposing major funding for assisting a third world nation.

Repeal of the Income Tax Codes and replacing it with a flat tax on earned personal income, investments and corporate earnings.

Repeal of all taxes levied by the US Government except for earned personal income, investments, corporate earnings and foreign imported goods.

Transfer of the Internal Revenue Service to OBFG.

Transfer of the Government Accounting Office to OBFG

Bringing our military forces home from Europe, Iraq, Afghanistan and Korea.

Class II

Military Base closings or re-openings

Immediate Deportation of all illegal immigrants

Setting limits on individuals campaign funding

Establishing shared cooperative ventures between government and private industry.

Wherever possible, personnel will be transferred from other agencies to fill the positions in the newly created OBFG. An example would be the transferring of former IRS investigators to the Investigative Group of DCOR. These personnel would be utilized to employ their skills in uncovering alleged improprieties being made by members of congress and other governmental agencies. If evidence is found, the investigation would be turned over to the Justice Department for action. No longer will we tolerate our government paying suppliers $75.00 for a standard hammer or $125.00 for a toilet seat.

The Analysis and Review Group will be responsible for reading and researching all new and pending legislation. They will present a summary of each bill to the Review Board. The Review Board will submit their recommendation to the Director, OBFG as to whether the bill should go to congress as a Class II action or deemed a Class I action to be voted on by popular vote of the people.

Once a bill is designated Class I, the Technical Support Group (TSG) will be responsible for preparing a power point summary presentation. This presentation will be made available for download to every county and parish web site. In this way, anyone who has a computer or access to a library computer can view the summary prior to voting on the bill.

Additionally, the TSG will be responsible for the development of a nationwide computer-voting network. This network will feature the latest in transmission security and simplicity at the voting booth. This network will be maintained on a separate secure site and used only for the popular vote of the people. The use of laptop computers by poling volunteers is envisioned as a new tool for assisting people to vote who can't travel to the polls due to age or disability.

The Procurement and Administrative Group (PAG) will provide the OBFG and all of its groups with administrative support. Additionally, PAG will have the added responsibility for interviewing and hiring dedicated, open-minded and highly intelligent individuals who have not been contaminated by the corruption in Congress.

The Oversight Branch of the Federal Government will set an impeccable standard for the other three branches to follow. They will shoulder no greater responsibility then insuring that Congress once again operates to support the will of the people.

CHAPTER 3

OUR FAILED CONGRESS

Our forefather's fervor and passion were instrumental in the establishment of our original Congress. They did this with the understanding that the representatives of the legislature would be responsible for supporting the will of the people. They must be rolling over in their graves at the sight of how corrupt and ineffective the modern Congress has become. Our forefathers thought that they had established a Constitution with built in checks and balances to keep the three branches of government in check. How could they have envisioned that a group of 550 men and women would rule uncontested over a population of more then three hundred ten million unhappy people and get away with it?

Today, most members of Congress support and vote for actions in accordance with their party's views. They have little or no interest on how their vote affects the common man or woman. Additionally, in some cases congressmen actually sell their votes to large corporations in return for sizeable contributions to their re-election campaign funds. Their agenda only calls for getting re-elected and making lots of money along the way.

Think back, do you know any of your friends who wanted us to give away our key manufacturing jobs as a result of NAFTA? I'm sure that a large majority of you will say **no.** But Congress disregarded the will of the people again and gave away many important jobs and now we are at record unemployment rates.

The same can be said about the war in Iraq. To this day, we have never found concrete proof that Iraq was even close to developing a nuclear weapon. Yet we went to war and still have troops in that country. Did the people of the United States want to go to war? The answer is clearly no. We are a peace-loving nation. Remember that it took the bombing of Pearl Harbor to get us involved in World War II.

"Despite a reluctance to go to war," once our troops were sent to Iraq, the nation immediately supported them and a quick victory was won. During March and April of 2003, we suffered 138 soldiers killed and 542 wounded. By the end of 2010 we had suffered 4,430 soldiers killed and 30,718 wounded. These figures are just for Iraq. Updated figures can be found on the web @ icasualties.org.

Once the battle was over, we should have pulled our troops out and sent them home. But at this point, the President and his advisers chose to stay and turn our elite combat troops into the role of policemen for which they were not properly motivated or trained. And since that time, the Congress has approved every military spending bill dealing with Iraq and Afghanistan. This wasted spending has cost the country to increase its debt by trillions of dollars. How can any Congressman face himself in a mirror and call himself a servant of the people.

According to Nobel Prize recipient Joseph Stiglitz and Harvard budget guru Linda Bilmes, the cost of the Iraq and Afghanistan wars have recently been revised upwards from 3 trillion dollars to from four to six trillion dollars as of today. In simple terms, each and every American now owes the Government approximately $44,000 towards the National Debt. The amount owed has almost doubled in the past eight years. This tells me that there is not one voice in Congress willing to show any leadership. And what has all of our military's futile effort and added financial debt gotten us? **WE**

**HAVE ENDURED NOTHING BUT MORE GRIEF AND
FINANCIAL BURDEN.** Doesn't anyone in Washington who
serves in a leadership capacity know how to spell **VIETNAM?**

Recently, the country was faced with legislation that
would have significantly increased taxes on personal income in
2011. These increases would have caused additional hardship
during a time of deep recession. Additionally, extended
unemployment benefits for nearly 10% of the workforce were
to end. We finally got a chance to see whom the politicians
serving in the Congress **really** work for. In both cases, the
Democrats and Republicans argued for their party's views
with <u>limited</u> compromise. Every time a reporter would make
reference to "the voice of the people," the congressman being
interviewed would immediately refer back to his party's line.
They clearly showed how unimportant that "We the People"
are to their agenda. No wonder we all feel helpless. **DO NOT
DISPARE AS HELP IS ON THE WAY.**

Let's face it, congressmen are like weather forecasters.
They can be wrong most of the time, but they are still secure
in their jobs. This is about to change. "We the People Party"
will make it change. When we finish, the days of the political
congressman will be history. True American patriots of our

new party will replace them. We will no longer be ruled by a majority of lawyers in Congress and the White House. The new breed will be passionate people from all walks of life who want to make a difference. These people will be selected from labor, education, law enforcement, health care and former military servicemen and women to make up the new ranks of Congress. Their goal will be to insure that the will of the people is served. These are the kind of patriots that we will put our trust in. They will be the ones that will shape our future of freedom and prosperity.

CHAPTER 4

PART TWO: THE FLAT TAX; MORE REVENUE FOR THE TREASURY-LESS TAXES PAID BY THE TAXPAYERS

A Flat Rate Income Tax For Everyone

In this chapter, we will examine the benefits of changing our current income tax system as we know it to a **Flat Rate Income Tax.** For simplicity, we will refer to this as the flat tax.

Each year, the Internal Revenue Service furnishes a free book to the public. This aid is entitled Publication 17 "Your Federal Income Tax." This book contains more than 300 pages of instructions, charts and illustrations necessary to fill out your individual form 1040 and any other required forms.

Preparation of personal taxes has become more challenging every year as tax laws keep changing. Soon everyone will need an accountant or tax preparation service to prepare his or her taxes. Everyone I have spoken with feel that our government needs to make a massive change in order to simplify filing taxes.

So how do we serve the will of the people? The answer is again a simple one. We need to establish a flat tax on all personal income. Wouldn't it be wonderful if 90 % or more of the taxpayers only had to file a one-page tax return? This is how we can end our income tax nightmare.

For 50 years or more, economists have been trying to convince the government that a fair flat rate income tax would generate significantly more revenue for expenditures than the current bracket system. In fact, it is felt that by establishing a rate of approximately thirty cents on every dollar earned, we could abolish almost all other taxes. The exceptions would be taxes on personal income, capital gains investments, corporate tax on profits and taxes on personal imported goods such as foreign automobiles manufactured outside of our country.

This would mean that everyone would pay at the same rate. Whether you are a billionaire or just working in a minimum wage job, you would pay the same rate of withholding tax. When it came time for filing your taxes, you would fill out a simple one-page form showing the total income from your W2 forms and 1099forms. You would then deduct your standard deduction and dependant allowances from your gross income to determine your adjusted gross income. There would be two charts on the back of the page. One chart would be for adjusted gross income under the poverty line. These people would receive a lessor tax rate. The other chart would be for everyone else. These charts would reflect the taxes due based on your adjusted gross income. You could then finish the form and file for your refund or to pay taxes due.

You would still need to use a separate form if you sold stock or bonds and turned a profit. You would owe the same rate as the flat tax on your investment gains. The other form required would be if you purchased personal foreign goods with a value exceeding $500, which were not manufactured in our country. We could establish a 40 or 50% added tax to the price of these goods unless they were production materials required for use in our factories. This tax would encourage us all to buy American made products.

Corporations and businesses would be taxed at a 20% rate on net profit. Every company would fall under the same flat tax rate. State auditors would conduct business audits annually to insure compliance by businesses located within their state.

Stiff fines would be levied for improprieties discovered and no loop holds would be permitted.

State Governments would be required to end all taxation in their state with the exception of property taxes. These taxes would continue to support services, schools and local government. The states would receive a portion of the withholding and corporate taxes generated within their state. This would likely come to 10 to 12 cents on the dollar.

Let's look at what we have just accomplished.

1) We have established a fair flat tax for all of our individual taxpayers.

2) We have streamlined filing of taxes for more then 90% of our taxpayers. In most cases only a one-page form will be required to file your individual taxes.

3) We have established a fair corporate and business tax on profits.

4) We have provided the states with money to run their state functions based on the volume of personal and corporate income generated in their states.

5) We have generated additional revenue from those who desire to purchase foreign goods instead of buying "American."

6) By streamlining the income tax filing system, we should significantly be able to reduce the number of employees working at the IRS.

7) And finally, we have been able to save the average American a lot of unwarranted tax expense by eliminating the following taxes.

   a) All Federal taxes except for personal income tax, interest on investments, corporate taxes and taxes on personal foreign goods items.

   b) All State taxes except for property taxes

   c) Sales Tax

   d) Liquor Tax

   e) Luxury Tax on U.S. goods

   f) Excise Taxes

   g) Cigarette Tax

   h) Medicare Tax

   i) Inventory Tax

   j) Real Estate Tax

   k) Well Permit Tax

   l) Fuel Permit Tax

m) Inheritance Tax

n) Road Usage Tax

o) CDL License Tax

p) Dog License Tax

q) Food License Tax

r) Vehicle Sales Tax

s) Gross Receipts Tax

t) Social Security Tax

u) Fishing License Tax

v) Building Permit Tax

w) Hunting License Tax

x) Marriage License Tax

y) Accounts Receivable Tax

z) Recreational Vehicle Tax

aa) Workers Compensation Tax

ab) Watercraft Registration Tax

ac) Telephone Usage Charge Tax

ad) Telephone State and Local Tax

ae) IRS Penalties (tax on top of tax)

af) State Unemployment Tax

ag) Federal Unemployment Tax

ah) Telephone Minimum Usage Surcharge Tax

ai) Telephone Federal Universal Service Fee Tax

aj) Gasoline Tax (almost 50 cents per gallon)

ak) Utility Taxes

al) Vehicle License Registration Tax

mm) Telephone Federal State and Local Surcharge Taxes

an) Telephone Recurring and Nonrecurring charges Tax

Wow, I think you'll agree that that's quite a list. Yet, I'm sure that there are many more taxes that I have missed. Now, we can see what using a little common sense will achieve. Eliminating these taxes will result in putting more of your hard-earned dollars back into your pocket.

The easiest way for Congress to deal with funding a new bill is to levy new taxes.

Instead of making a cut in the monstrous government budget, they dig deeper into our pockets. This method of taxation must be ended for good.

When "We the People Party" take our government back, the party's representatives in Congress will work for the people's best interest. They will correct all of the injustices that we have had to endure. **HELP IS ON THE WAY.**

CHAPTER 5

PART THREE: REVIVING THE ECONOMY, CREATING NEW JOBS AND PRODUCTS

Reviving Our Economy

The time has come to take positive steps to create meaningful and well paying jobs for our unemployed. One of the major goals of the "We the People Party" will be to achieve full employment as soon as possible.

Those of us who lived during WWII can look back and remember how our nation banded together and produced war materials for not only our army but for our allies also. Winston Churchill referred to us as the "Arsenal of Democracy". Our manufacturing plants rapidly retooled and soon produced vast amounts of ships, tanks, aircraft, artillery, rifles, and everything down to and including clothing. This was accomplished in record time. We must once again call on the American people to pull together and whenever possible buy our **American made goods.**

The first thing that we must do is to repeal NAFTA and bring our lost production jobs back to America. Then we must establish tight controls on what we import from other countries. Any item that can be manufactured in the USA should be made here. As an example, we should put our textile mills on a seven-day workweek, while they begin producing the woven and knitted materials needed for our clothing. The added hours would create many new jobs at the mills. Additional jobs would be required by the clothing manufacturers in order to meet the demands.

A few years ago, we bailed out the big three automobile manufacturers from financial ruin. Now it's payback time. We must require that these manufacturers use only parts that are manufactured in the United States for their new automobiles. Additionally, the "Big Three" will be required to partner with our government engineers in the development of new fuel-efficient engines. Initially, these engines will be designed for full size automobiles, SUVs and light trucks. Criteria for these engines will be that they must attain speeds of at least 80 MPH and get between 50 to 60 miles per gallon of gas on the highway. These engines will be given no more then 24 months to complete this project.

Once this project is complete, this team of engineers will use the same technology and develop new engines for all models of US made vehicles manufactured over the past 10 years. This will give all of us the option as to whether we want to spend $30,000 to $50,000 on the purchase of a new vehicle or have a new engine installed in their old vehicle for approximately $5,000. Either way, the purchasers will have doubled or tripled their gas mileage over their previous engines. Additionally, just think of the number of new jobs that will be created in order to meet the demand for these new engines. This does not include additional new jobs required for the installation of the new engines.

Just think of the overall reduction in fossil fuel that our country will save. Also, if the government removes all taxes from vehicle fuel, as a result of the flat tax, we could again see gas prices drop below $2.00 per gallon.

Next, we need to repair our roads and bridges. I am aware of a very special group of dedicated government employees who work at the National Institute of Health in Bethesda, MD. They work in the field of nanotechnology. This means that they are able to develop new compounds by combining different forms of matter. One of their projects has been to develop a road surface that will require no maintenance for one hundred years. If this becomes possible, then think of the possibilities. If they were to install solar panels, large storage batteries and heating wires within the surface of the road there would never be a problem with snow or ice on the roads. In the plains states where it is always windy, it might be more efficient to use electric producing windmills for power.

I have already been informed that some union officials are protesting to their congressmen about this new material. They feel that using it will reduce road construction jobs in the future. I have one thing to say to these union officials: your job has always been to insure that your members are being treated fairly by their employers. Be forewarned that "We the People Party" will not allow your interference with the forward progress of our country. So step aside, or join in our movement to create a better country for all of us.

Now we will address the illegal immigrant situation. The optimum word is **<u>illegal.</u>** I fail to understand why Congress and the Administration refuse to act regarding this problem. These illegal immigrants are in this country in violation of our laws. Many of them receive health care benefits. Others are employed and taking jobs away from our unemployed workers.

Therefore, I call on the President and Congress to take immediate steps to **locate and deport** all illegal immigrants. If you do not respond to this request, you are all guilty of aiding and abetting a known crime. And don't think that that won't become an issue in the next upcoming election.

I am still waiting for the President to live up to his campaign pledge to bring our military forces home from Iraq and Afghanistan. If and when they ever get back to the US, they should be deployed to tighten the security of our two borders. Army troops are already trained and equipped for this type of mission. By employing sensors, ground radar and night vision equipment, we can greatly restrict the flow of drugs over our borders and stop illegal immigrants right at the border. Of even more importance is the apprehension of terrorists who may attempt to cross these borders.

I consider this a very good mission for the returning Army troops. Rather than disband all of the returning Divisions, some units can immediately assume this roll. Unit integrity is a very important consideration when giving the Army a mission.

The Army will be able to deploy units down to fire-team level (4 or 5 men with two vehicles).

Once we start manufacturing again, we will quickly reduce our unemployment. I am not concerned what world opinion thinks of us. If we need to approach isolationism, then so be it. Many countries will become upset with us because we are taking our jobs back and we currently buy their goods. This must stop and our rallying cry must be **"Buy American."**

CHAPTER 6

Open Letter to Our President

November 5, 2010

Dear Mister President,

I am writing this letter to you in order to discuss major concerns that I have regarding the leadership of our country.

Let me first say that I voted for you. Your stand on the issues during your campaign gave me hope that finally we would have a President that would change the downward spiral of our county. Unfortunately, you have wasted the first two years of your term in office. You have let the advantage of having a Democratic Congress pass you by. Now if you are to achieve any measure of success, you will have to do it on your own merit.

It would help if you listened more to the voice of the people. The intelligent ones will tell you to place your healthcare bill on hold. We just can't afford the additional taxes that will be levied to support this program. If you had honored your pledge by bringing our servicemen and women home shortly after you took office, the burden of healthcare might have had a chance.

Now after spending more then a trillion dollars on the wars in Iraq and Afghanistan since you have been in office, we are watching as the National Debt increases daily. It is apparent to me that your advisers have not learned anything from our country's venture into Vietnam. Will you and your staff ever get fiscal responsibility under control? At the rate you are going the answer is **NO.**

Do you want to leave office with the legacy of being the first black President to lead his country into **bankruptcy?** I hope not, because you were not responsible for starting it. This dubious distinction belongs solely with your predecessor. So here are a few things that you can do to stop this trend.

First, bring home all of our troops from around the globe. In Europe, I would suggest leaving a few equipment pools with vehicles for one Armored Division. We would need to furnish only maintenance personnel to maintain and exercise the engines on a regular basis. Then, we could arrange to have brigade size maneuvers once each year with French and German units to keep our alliance strong. This would also give the Air Force an opportunity to test its airlift and re-supply capabilities.

In Korea, we should pull all of our troops and equipment out now. It is a complete waste of budget resources. If North Korea ever invades the country of South Korea again; the United Nations will swiftly deal with it.

In dealing with Afghanistan and Iraq, you should issue an executive order to the Department of Defense giving them 120 days to withdraw **all troops, supplies and equipment** for immediate return to the continental limits of the United States. Also, issue a warning order to the Commanding Generals of the combat elements. It should state that upon re-entering the US these troops will be earmarked for providing border security to our two borders.

Now, you will have ended the expense of war along with its casualties. The new task for our servicemen and women will be fulfilling a mission of great importance to our nation.

This next task is a tough one, but that's why you are our President. The will of the people demands that **all** illegal immigrants in this country be rounded up and deported. Many of them hold down jobs that could be filled by our legal population. In this time of record unemployment, it is impossible to justify any illegal immigrant being given preferential treatment over our citizens.

If you really want to go down as one of our greatest Presidents, who served his country and his people with honor, then here are a few things that you can do.

1)   Repeal NAFTA and review our trade agreements in order to restore as many of the production jobs that we have lost over the past years as possible. Increase tariffs on foreign goods so that we can produce similar products and sell American made goods to the public. This will also act to increase employment.

2)   Support the voice the people in their attempt to use the **"popular vote"** for all legislation that affects the country as a whole. You are our President. Do you have the intestinal fortitude to take a stance and support the will of the people? If so, you will rank with the founders of our country as a man of historic vision.

3) Support the voice of the people in their proposal to add a fourth branch of government to the Constitution of the United States. This new addition will be called the Oversight Branch of the Federal Government. This branch will serve as the checks and balances for our **"Runaway Congress."** The only way that you can control Congress is by your veto. Both Congress and the President often pass major legislation and spending bills with total disregard for the will of the people. This must stop now. Therefore, the Oversight Branch will determine if a bill is to be voted on by popular vote or is a routine action that can be dealt with by Congress.

4) Create a new Crime Bill that will have teeth in it. It should contain stiffer penalties dealing with drugs, repeat offenders, rape and murder. Also, you should declare that organized gangs are illegal and must be disbanded immediately. They do not qualify under law as peaceful assembly. Instead, they are criminal in nature and undermine the very foundation of freedom. And finally, reduce the policy of "three strikes and you're out," to **"ONE STRIKE AND YOU'RE OUT FOR GOOD."**

If you can achieve this, you will go down as the greatest President since Abraham Lincoln and you will become the champion of the people.

A Patriot of the People,

Dale Howard Wright

CHAPTER 7

Reviving the Draft

As we take steps to balance the budget in future years, we will need to reduce the size of our standing army. We are no longer at war. When we pull most of our Army units back home, they will be the hardest hit in the reduction in forces. In order to keep our active Army units at combat readiness, we will need to keep them at, or near, full strength.

In order to do this, I propose that we revive the draft with the following changes. First, **all** high school seniors will be eligible for the draft upon graduation unless they are accepted into an accredited full time College. They will have to be 17 years of age or older and pass the physical exam to qualify for the draft. They will only serve one year on active duty instead of the old system of two years. Any male leaving school without graduating will qualify for the draft upon reaching his 17th birthday. College students will be exempt until they graduate. If they are dropped from the rolls of the school or quit, they will immediately be reported to the draft board. Upon graduation from College, they will also be eligible for one year of service under the draft. The college graduate will have the choice of serving one year in the ranks or applying for Officer Candidate School where if he earns a commission, he will incur an extra year of service.

In utilizing this system, we can provide the recruits necessary to provide fillers to our combat elements. As an added bonus, we will have a substantial number of our countrymen trained for military service should we ever be called upon to mobilize again.

There is one more factor that must be considered. Our country is getting soft. When I was a teenager, I spent most of my free time playing baseball or basketball with my classmates. We were all in very good physical shape. So when I joined the Army after graduating from high school, I adjusted well to the discipline and physical training.

Has anyone looked at the average physical condition of the male high school junior or senior? Most of them are overweight and desperately in need of physical exercise. Military training will whip them into shape and also instill in them a respect for authority, developing teamwork with others and taking self-pride in their personal achievements.

Reviving the military draft will keep our country's overall defensive posture in good stead for centuries to come. Military service will also help mold our young men into the leaders of tomorrow. **This is definitely a Win Win situation.**

CHAPTER 8

PART FOUR: GREATLY REDUCING CRIME THROUGH HARSHER TREATMENT OF CONVICTED CRIMINALS

A Tough New Brand of Criminal Justice

Those of you who lived in the 1940's will remember that we almost never locked the doors of our home. It was safe for women to walk alone outside after dark. The only crime that we read about in the newspapers was about the Feds arresting some member of the syndicate for laundering money. Well, coming from Chicago, there were always complaints about the Democrats stuffing the ballot box, but that was never proved.

Today things are quite different. Crime is ramped. Gangs have taken over our inner cities. Major crimes like violent assault, rape, and murder are common every day occurrences in almost every mid-sized city. When a crime is committed, witnesses often are afraid to testify because they receive death threats.

Drugs are a major cause of crime. The drug cartels can easily transport drugs over our unprotected borders. And when law enforcement does apprehend the drug dealers they get a slap on the wrist by some lenient judge. Somehow the courts have adopted a policy that gives criminals short or no jail time for their first two offences. Then, they get time in jail on the third conviction. **What kind of justice is this?**

Our society is continually being asked to furnish new modern jails. This is money that we should **never spend on convicted criminals.** So here is how we should rid ourselves of the ever-increasing number of felons in our country.

Establishing a Penal Colony

For those of you who have never heard of a penal colony, let me explain. As late as the 1930s some European countries selected islands where they sent their convicted criminals. In most cases, they used them for forced labor. The conditions were very primitive and few ever survived their sentences.

I feel that we should change our laws so that **anyone convicted of a felony** would automatically lose his or her citizenship and be directly sent to the penal colony for the rest of their life.

In order to establish an ideal setting for this colony, our country should locate a small island in the Pacific Ocean that is at least 500 miles from any populated area. The only features that the island must have is that it be uninhabited, have fresh drinking water and soil suitable for farming. If necessary, we can purchase this island from the country that owns it.

Initially, we will deliver a three-month supply of foodstuffs to last the first batch of criminals until they can plant and grow a large garden. Garden tools, seeds, fishing hooks and lines will be furnished. Monthly, a converted Navy prison ship will deliver a new batch of prisoners with more seeds to increase the size of their gardens.

Then, once a year, a new set of garden tools, clothing, and seeds will be delivered to the island. It may seem cruel to make them live this way. However, in actuality they will enjoy much more freedom then they would have in jail. Just the thought of spending the rest of their life on an island with no contact to the outside world, should definitely make potential criminals think twice before they attempt to commit a felony.

One might think that it would be easy to escape from the island. If the prisoners tried to build a boat, everyone would want to escape in it. How far would they get without sufficient food or water? And, if a boat or seaplane tried to rescue someone, it would wind up the survival of the fittest. Without citizenship, where could they go to be accepted? Definitely not in the USA.

My goal is to rid our country of its convicted felons. In doing so, we will save tens of millions of dollars each year by not having to pay for their incarceration expenses.

I also make no differentiation between male and female felons. **<u>They all will be sent to the penal colony together for life.</u>**

Changes to Regular Jail Time

I advocate taking away all of the privileges that convicted criminals other then felons receive while they are in jail serving their sentences. Right now, we treat criminals in jail better then we do our honest hard working low-income citizens. Why should we pamper inmates with TVs, libraries and athletic equipment? Being in jail should not be a pleasant experience.

Those sentenced to jail will get plenty of exercise making small rocks from large ones, scrubbing floors and toilets and being taught discipline. In many cases, they will have an opportunity to work in a prison workshop manufacturing license plates or selected products for the military.

I do condone monthly visits by family members provided that the inmate has caused no trouble during the month.

I also fail to see why we the people should have to foot the bill for the inmate's expenses, i.e. food, clothing, toilet articles and annual dental checks. We should require the inmate's family to pay his or her bill in full before they can be released. Inmates who produce excellent products in the prison workshops, will receive wage credits to be credited against their final bill. Inmates who can't satisfy payment of their final bill will be placed on a chain gang for up to six months before being released.

By ridding ourselves of all of our convicted felons, there should never be a need to build new jails in our lifetime.

CHAPTER 9

ENDING GANG TERRORISM

Today we are faced with more crime then at any time in the history of our nation. It is apparent that law enforcement and the court system are not acting together in support of the will of the people. We **want and demand** a crime free environment in which to raise our families. We **all have the basic right** to live in a secure atmosphere where crime is miniscule and freedom and personal safety is the norm. So how do we achieve these goals?

First, we must identify the major reasons for the existence of so much crime in our country. The answers are very simple. We have allowed disruptive groups to form within our society that are today's gangs. Whether they are riding motorcycles or walking the streets of every large city in our nation, their goals are to intimidate and subvert our population. They bully us, assault us, and in some cases rape and murder our citizens. Their income comes from muggings, theft of personal property and the sale of drugs.

Since the early days of the Federal Bureau of Investigation, the FBI has been entrusted with identifying and arresting all known subversive groups that endanger our way of life. Until now, they have been successful in controlling the criminals and bank robbers of the 1930's, German spies both before and during WWII, communist spies during the cold war and now terrorist cells like those that caused the despicable acts on 9/11.

I am confident that the FBI has files containing the names of the leaders of at least 90% of the gangs in the United States. Now we need the Supreme Court to rule that all of these gangs are subversive organizations and must be disbanded. Membership in this kind of illegal assembly will carry with it a penalty of life imprisonment and loss of citizenship for this felony. Since this will be a federal crime, one conviction in federal court and the guilty will be sent to the Penal Colony for the remainder of their life. This type of strict law enforcement will break up the hard core gangs and allow law enforcement to concentrate on other serious issues such as the illegal sale and use of drugs.

The weak link in the criminal justice system is the failure of some federal judges to severely sentence criminals who have been found guilty of their crimes. These weak judges must be disbarred and replaced with new ones who will be committed to ending crime. The new policy must be **One Strike and You Are Out.**

CHAPTER 10

Marching Ahead With New Technology

During the 1940's and into the 1960's our country's engineers, designers and inventors came forth with new labor saving devices and convenience items that are looked on today as routine necessities. If you lived during this time, you can remember experiencing TV for the first time. Then, came panty hose. In cars, we began seeing directional signals, seat belts and air bags. Our clothing began being made from artificial fibers like polyester. As the years progressed, so did technology. Today, many appliances like microwave ovens, garbage disposals and personal computers have all become part of our daily lives.

Our nation's technicians must continue to invent labor saving devices that the whole world will want and need. Government and industry must come together and partnership in producing new and enhanced equipment and processes. One essential way this can be done is to develop new internal combustion engines that will increase gas mileage from 50 to

60 miles per gallon in standard motor vehicles. Then, using the same technology, go back ten model years and produce similar engines so that owners can replace the old gas guzzling ones with the new fuel efficient ones. This would also greatly reduce our dependence on foreign oil.

These are the types of ideas that we must explore. New and/or updated technology will also produce many new good paying jobs. The rapid growth of our nation's economy will be governed by the volume of goods that we can produce for both our country and world use.

CHAPTER 11

Military Veterans "Stand Up and be Counted"

The time has come for all Americans to peacefully reclaim their country. We have no other recourse but to force the will of the people on our belligerent government. This can, and will, be done by using our votes for "We the People Party's" candidates in the 2012 elections.

My fellow veterans, who better to assume the leadership role of this great nation then those of us who have faithfully served our country in peace and war? We are the patriots who have sacrificed and shed our own blood so that the American way may be preserved. Now we must again band together and use our military organizational skills to insure that the voice of the common man is heard and acted upon.

The Congress and Administration have led us in a downward spiral until we are at the doorstep of total disaster. **We no longer have the luxury of sitting by and letting our**

elected officials in Washington play guessing games with our future. We must act, and act <u>NOW,</u> to insure our birthright, in addition to that of our children.

These are critical times and we must all band together to affect peaceful change. By forming a coalition, consisting of our veteran's organizations, we can develop a party of the common man that will become invincible in numbers at the voting booth. In this manner, we will be able to unseat the inept and disloyal government officials from office. We will target and replace these congressmen with qualified and dedicated <u>patriots.</u> Our selected candidates will correct the injustices that have been wrought on the people. In our ranks we have an abundance of outstanding potential leaders, who will once again take command and make our country strong.

Today, more then ever before, our nation needs the wisdom and leadership that its veterans can provide. Here is one area that we are all experts in. We know how to follow an operations plan to successful completion. So here is what I propose:

In Chapter 1, I spoke about organizing a new party named "We the People Party." Most politicians and our failed congressional representatives are probably laughing at the notion of trying to organize such a movement from grass roots level. But if we as veterans band together and lend our time and talents to this plan, we will succeed in replacing many of the ineffective members of Congress in the 2012 election.

Once we organize and unite in our goals, our party will control a majority of the popular vote. Our newly elected representatives to Congress will then insure that fiscal control is once again restored to the government and that the will of the people is acted upon.

By gaining a foothold in Congress, we will insure that wasteful Government spending is brought to a screeching halt. We will work hard at balancing the budget. We will insure that our military forces are utilized efficiently and not spread out all over the world. We will continue to insure that the Government's contracts with its military and veterans are honored. These contracts include, equal pay for comparable civilian jobs in the active military, continuation of the current military retirement system, no reductions in healthcare programs such as Tri-Care for Life, and continued support and funding for the VA. Veterans Affairs programs will be monitored closely to insure that not one single disabled veteran ever sees a reduction in his monthly services or pay check.

To achieve these lofty goals and stop the wasteful spending of our country's resources, we must organize without further delay. We will need to enlist volunteers to develop our state and county/parish focal points. We will need the volunteer service and wisdom of legal minds, accountants, advertising consultants, web site developers, and party organizers.

Therefore, I make a special call to you, my former Vietnam era veterans, to come forward and serve your country once again with the honor that you have shown in the past. Only this time you will control your destiny and we will be allowed to win. Many of us are now retired and have the time to devote to saving our country from ruin. We must come to the aid of our country once more. Volunteer your talents and services. Show your fellow countrymen that you want to insure the "American Way of Life." I assure you that if you do, they will eagerly join us.

As patriots, we will always represent the voice of the people. We will succeed in achieving our goals of making America free of debt. We will establish a smaller but efficient government that supports the will of the people. Along the way, we will develop an economy that is rich in wealth and prosperity. This will be our legacy.

Contact me. Share your thoughts and ideas. This is a huge endeavor. I need your help in getting organized. We need enthusiastic supporters. No volunteer will be turned away. Once I find qualified leaders, who passionately embrace our goals, I will pass the reigns to them. I still intend to help in any way that I can to insure that this time we win this crucial battle.

I have started an email address at wethepeopleparty@ charter.net. What we need first is to find volunteers to help in developing a web site. This site will be our principle means of communicating with our membership. Next we will need to find leaders who are willing to serve as state and county organizers. Then, we will need to find volunteers to start enlisting voters to our cause.

If anyone has any doubts that we can have a greater impact then the other political parties, consider these facts. There are approximately 213 million legal voters in the United States. During the last presidential election, only 133 million people voted. We have more then 23 million living veterans in the US. Therefore, if only 50% of us voted and each veteran convinced five of his family members or friends to also vote for our candidates, we would sweep any future election. Remember, this time, the people's vote will count. Together we will lift our country out of debt and return the nation to its former greatness.

Time is getting critical. We must organize now. The sooner we do, the sooner we start winning congressional seats and possibly even the presidency. Then we can truly return the country to the people.

CHAPTER 12

Government Regulation—Good or Bad for Us

For most of my adult life, I have believed in free enterprise and that the market place would make adjustments without government intervention. However, as one gets older he becomes wiser and views things in a new light. I now think that **limited** government regulation in our economy may be necessary for the good of the people. So let's take a look at an example of where regulation would be beneficial for our nation's economy.

Credit Cards

Most of us own one or more credit cards. The **bank debit card** is a very useful item. We can shop for our personal necessities such as food, gas, clothing and items for our home without having to carry large quantities of cash on our person. Purchases made using these cards are automatically deducted from existing funds located in our bank accounts.

The other card is the **standard credit card.** This card is very useful for larger purchases, vacations and unexpected expenses. These cards can be very useful as long as you are able to pay off the balance over a short period of time. Unfortunately, many Americans, especially those with younger families, are unable to pay off these balances. Then in hard times of unemployment, prolonged illness and rising cost of goods and services, these families have no other recourse but to run their cards up to the limit. These are not bad people. They are just trying to survive.

So here is what our so-called **friendly bankers** do. They raise the interest rates on their cards to further cripple those who have high balances. They try to justify these rate increases by claiming that many cardholders are not making their payments or going into bankruptcy. In essence, they want those of us who have been good account holders to pay for their losses. Today, these lending institutions have raised their annual interest rates on their credit cards to 25% or higher. In my eyes this constitutes **Usury.**

It is common knowledge that the banks are very liberal in their approval of credit card applications. A week doesn't go by that I don't receive credit card applications with pre-approved limits of $5000 or more on each one. Many middle class people have taken advantage of these offers. However, they now find themselves getting deeper in debt as the annual rates on their cards have almost doubled. **This is a perfect place for limited government regulation to come to the aid of the people. The Congress should immediately pass legislation that will set the maximum rate for credit cards at prime rate plus 2%. This percentage would be adjusted annually on January 1 either up or down.**

It is very doubtful that any bank will stop issuing credit cards as a result of this new restriction. After all, where would they find another **"goose that lays golden eggs"** to replace the profits that they presently receive from their credit card business?

This should be a no-brainer for the Congress. The tens of millions of dollars saved by our people as a result of lowering credit card interest will be spent in the market place. Thus we will be further stimulating the economy.

We know that Congress recently was cowered into bailing out the banking industry. This act was again taken without the support of the people. Now Congress has an opportunity to act in support of the people by restricting interest rates on credit cards. Will they help the people in their time of need or will they again fail to support the needs of their fellow countrymen?

CHAPTER 13

Proposals that Will Greatly Aid in Balancing the Budget

Throughout this book, I have offered solutions to many problems that our country is facing today. During my thought process I always kept in mind, "how can I reduce the cost of eliminating the problem and still provide for the will of the people?"

I have prepared a chart showing these proposals and whether they will add cost or savings to the annual budget. This chart is shown at Tab C. One item that I didn't discuss in this book is the downsizing of our government. This would take a complete new second book to address all of the cuts that I would propose in our overstaffed Federal Government. However, this can, and must, be done soon. But first, "We the People Party" must win the majority seats in congress. Then we can finish cleaning house in accordance with the will of the people.

It will be for you the common man and woman to decide your destiny. Are you ready to make your vote count so that we can once again regain the freedom given to us by our forefathers? If you are sick of being oppressed by the burden of unjust taxation and corruption in our government, please give us your vote. If you are tired of feeling that nobody can help us with your plight, please give us your vote. If you want to become a modern day Patriot, please tell your friends and family that we are their last chance to preventing the country from going into financial ruin, please ask them to join us and give us their vote.

TOGETHER WE WILL REGAIN OUR LOST HERITAGE. WE WILL ONCE AGAIN DISPLAY THE PASSION OF OUR FOREFATHERS. AND WHEN WE GO TO BED AT NIGHT, OUR PRAYERS WILL BE OF THANKS FOR AGAIN GIVING US BACK OUR FREEDOM.

MAJOR COST CUTTING PROPOSALS (TAB C)

PROPOSAL	Annual Savings / Budge Expense
Replace the current income tax code with the proposed flat-tax rate on all earned income	Potential for billions of dollars in new revenue each year for the US Treasury.
New technology – Fuel efficient engines.	Hundreds of millions of dollars in new revenues for the auto industry.
Establishing a Penal Colony system for all of our nations convicted criminals who are found guilty of felony crimes.	Initial expense for purchase of an island location. Thereafter, tens of millions of dollars saved annually.
End our participation in the wars in Iraq and Afghanistan and bring the troops home.	Savings of more then 500 billion dollars annually.
Bring home our troops from Europe and South Korea.	Savings of billions of dollars.
Establish the new "Oversight Branch of the Federal Government. Wherever available, personnel will be transferred from other departments in the government.	Annual expenses unkown

CHAPTER 14

The Rebirth of a Mighty Nation

We have now reached a point in history where the fate of our once proud nation rests in the balance. Either we take positive action to prevent future bankruptcy and another serious depression from happening, or we sit idly by and go down like the Titanic.

I, for one, am going to do everything within my power to prevent this from happening. I have proposed a plan whereby we can end the belligerent attitude of our members in Congress and save our country from a major catastrophic meltdown. Congress and the Administration have been found guilty of bringing our country to the brink of bankruptcy. They have totally distanced themselves from the voice of the people. It seems that the only way that they can accomplish anything anymore is to add new and crippling tax burdens on our people.

We all feel the pain of our shrinking incomes. We feel helpless because it appears that no help is in sight. **But there is a solution.** It is time that we all use our most powerful weapon to restore our freedom and make lasting changes that will set us on the road to recovery. This weapon is our **VOTE. WE MUST ALL BAND TOGETHER AND USE THESE VOTES AGAINST THOSE WHO HAVE DESTROYED OUR HERITAGE.**

There are some new independent parties that have recently formed. Their goals are commendable, but they fail to see the big picture. Our government needs a complete overhaul, void of **politics and politicians.** The only way to achieve this is to completely **vote the Congress and the Administration out of office.** This **can and will be done** by voting for the candidates of our new "We the People Party."

With the support of our military veterans and other patriotic members of the party, we will build an invincible organization that will defeat all of the political candidates from the other parties. In future elections, our slate of candidates will continue to sustain our overwhelming majority in the Congress and the Administration because we answer to the voice of the people. No political party will ever achieve this much Power.

So what are our new party's principle goals?

1) Restore fiscal control to a budget that is designed to meet the needs of the people.

2) Repeal any bill that has cost us jobs as a result of foreign trade

3) Seal our borders to prevent illegal immigration and drug trafficking

4) Deport all illegal immigrants

5) Bring all of our troops home

6) Establish a new branch of government to serve as a check and balance over Congress

7) Establish the popular vote for all major legislation involving the citizens of our great nation

8) Institute a fair flat tax on earned income, profit on investments and corporate profits

9) Abolish all other taxes except for property taxes and foreign purchases over five hundred dollars.

10) Stiffen punishment for those convicted of crimes

11) Balance the Federal budget and strive to pay off the national debt within twenty years

12) Develop a voting base of 60 million voters for our slate of candidates in the 2012 presidential election.

13) Continue to build our membership base in order to assure that our future candidates are elected to the Congress. In this way, the will of the people will always be served.

14) RESPOND TO THE WILL OF THE PEOPLE

When we achieve these goals, we will have successfully brought about the **Rebirth of our Mighty Nation** and the United States of America will once again show the world how democracy works.

NOW IT IS YOUR TURN TO STAND UP AND BE COUNTED

I have given you a peaceful plan of action that will restore our freedom to the people of America. **This is our last chance. You can no longer sit idly by and say,"Things will get better."** If you think this way, then you have sealed your fate and that of your friends and family. **Now is the time to stand up for what you know is right. All you need to do is give us your vote in the 2012 federal elections.** By doing so you will become part of the largest movement in our country's history and you will go down as a true **AMERICAN PATRIOT.**

Remember that our new party is non-political. We are here to support the will of the people. Once we regain control of the Congress and Administration, there will never again be any secret deals made that the public is not aware of. We will prosecute any official who is caught taking contributions of any kind from corporate entities. If the people are satisfied with the accomplishments of our new Congress, our congressional representatives will be assured of being re-elected over and over again.

Our candidates will be chosen from all walks of life. They will be truly qualified in the fields of economics, law, labor, industry, engineering, medical, education, retired military and law enforcement. We all will have a chance to read the biography of each candidate, and then choose the ones we desire to be placed on our slate for the next federal election. When you register with the party, you will be given a party number. This number is all that you will need to cast your votes on our web site.

If you should decline to become a member of our new party, remember your vote at the polls in support of our candidates is **<u>still the most important decision</u>** that you will ever make. Give us your vote and together **we will all make our county strong again.**

      In closing, I wish to extend a personal invitation for you and your friends to join us on this historic march in once again making our government responsive to the will of the people. I assure you that it is a wonderful feeling knowing that you are working as a patriot to restore freedom to the people. We are asking that all-new members remit a registration fee of $5.00 to defray our administrative costs. This fee represents a one-time charge and entitles you to a lifetime membership in the party. In return, you will receive a beautiful patriotic campaign pin and your laminated membership card and number. We hope that you will proudly wear the pin or display it prominently.

      As soon as possible, we hope to have our web site up and running. This will also give you a running count of our current membership. Of more importance, your membership number will allow you vote for your choice of our party's slate of candidates using this web site.

      A registration form for each new member should be filled out and returned with your remittance. This form is shown in the next chapter and may be reproduced locally.

Please mail your remittance to "We the People Party," P.O.Box 8166, Janesville, Wisconsin 53547-8166. You may also feel free to email me at <u>wethepeopleparty@charter.net</u> with your questions or comments.

Join this patriotic movement today. Become a modern day Patriot. Your children and grandchildren will someday thank you for standing up and restoring their freedom.

CHAPTER 15

"WE THE PEOPLE" Party
Registration Form

I wish to join the "We the People Party." It is my intention to vote for my party's slate of candidates at the next general election. I share the party's goals to insure that freedom is once again restored to the people of this once mighty nation.

Upon receipt of this registration form for membership in the We the People Party, you will receive a beautiful party campaign button and a laminated card with your membership number. This will allow you to submit your choice of your party's candidates for state and federal government positions. These votes will be cast on our web site.

Name_____

Home Address _____

City/State/Zip _____

Email Address _____

Please mail this registration form along with a $5.00 administrative fee to:

"WE THE PEOPLE" Party
PO BOX 8166
Janesville, Wisconsin 53547-8166

"GOD BLESS AMERICA"

REMEMBER, THAT THIS IS <u>YOUR</u> LAST CHANCE TO
SAVE AMERICA. ACT NOW TO BECOME A

<u>TRUE PATRIOT</u>

<u>"GOD BLESS AND SAVE AMERICA"</u>